the Way to Peace

A message from God that will transform your life

MICHELLE SINCLAIR

the Way to Peace

For information about this title or to order other books and/or electronic media, contact the publisher:
Michelle Sinclair
Oxbow, Saskatchewan, Canada
Michelleesinclair@icloud.com

ISBN: 978-1-9990676-01 (print)
978-1-9990676-25 (eBook)
978-1-9990676-18 (audio)

Printed in the United States of America

Cover and Interior design: 1106 Design

Table of Contents

About the Author

The Quote that Changed My Life

"A bird born in a cage thinks that flying is a disease."

—Alejandro Jordorowsky

If you have ever started to question a long-held belief that you have, there is always that first initial thought: that thing you heard or that idea that came to your mind or was posed from someone else that starts it all. That starts the questioning. That either makes your beliefs start to crumble and lead to more questions, which ultimately leads you to something new. It may also solidify what you believe and makes it even stronger. For me it was a simple quote, a quote that would change everything—my beliefs and my ideas of what was and what was not reality for me. The quote was simple, yet to the point; and when I read it I felt like I was almost immediately set free from the limiting chains that had bound me for my whole life to that point, with the exception of the first few years of my life. At that time, I am sure I still had some recollection of God's true nature. This quote would change not only my beliefs, but change me as a person, and began a transformation that ultimately lead me to freedom and truth. It set me free of the fears I carried about, even questioning what it was I believed. Through this questioning and change I was led to my purpose, my true calling.

Once our perception is changed we realize there is no going back, like a puppy refusing to be put back inside a box. When the outside world and all its possibilities have been seen, who would ever want to live in a box?

So why do we even have these beliefs in the first place? How do we know which ones are true and which ones are not? Have you ever heard the phrase or Bible verse, "You will know the truth and the truth will set you free?" For me this rings true. Through my work with clients, I see the freedom that comes when false beliefs are released. For example, when we believe things about ourselves that are not true, we do not feel free. Beliefs like "I am not good enough," "worthy enough," "smart enough," "liked enough," etc., do not feel like freedom. Simply put, it is because these things are not and have never been true, even if they feel true. When you let go of these false beliefs and replace them with the truth, you truly do set yourself free. I, however, am not talking about personal feelings of self when I say I changed. I am talking about the false beliefs I had about God.

As a child, I always felt a closeness to God. I felt as though God really listened to me and did what I asked. I have always really loved God. This may make me sound like I was a wonderful child. I wasn't.

I was raised in an extremely religious home where we attended church twice on Sundays, said prayers before every meal, read the Bible Christmas morning and never believed in Santa Claus because that took away from the meaning of Christmas. None of these things I enjoyed.

I did, however, love God. As a young child, a close friend of my family's can recall me running around the church basement at top speeds only to stop and run over to her lap, look her straight in the eyes and say, "You know, people without Jesus really suffer." Then just as quickly I rushed off and kept running with the other kids. I knew we suffered when we felt unloved, and Jesus to me was that symbol of love.

As children, we had fear preached into us. We were told how demons dress up like angels in disguise, so we must always be on the lookout for evil, as it lurked everywhere. This for me created a lot of fear. We were also told how lucky we were to be born into the right religion and how sad it was that others were not and would have to suffer in hell. How sad to believe more than half the world was going to suffer in hell. We did not learn about other religions unless it was to point out their faults. Reading about other religions could cause doubt in us and create questions. This might lead us astray and into the arms of the devil, who was just waiting to scoop us up and take us to hell.

I don't know about you, but believing that the consequences of not believing exactly what I was told to believe would lead me to hell was compelling enough to not question anything and just blindly believe what I had been told. It is actually quite amazing to me, knowing my personality, that I went for so long believing the way that I did. When I grew up, I went as far as shutting out messages from God because I was scared they were a trick! When I had my eyes opened, everything changed.

I have always had a strong pull toward needing to know the truth. I could see the truth clearly most of the time and could tell when I was being lied to or if someone wasn't being genuine in who they said they were. This was such a necessary part of my life. I realized that in my search for the truth the things I suffered in this life were for a reason, and these reasons were all for the greater good. It led me to be able to fulfill my purpose here on Earth.

Through the suffering I brought on myself in my teenage and young adult years, I learned. I grew. I became me. We could all hide under our guilt and shame and let our lives be guided this way. I could have chosen this for myself. I could have lived life as a victim, but I did not.

We are all unique. We all have our own story that makes us who we are. All our stories are important and beautiful in their own way. No one is less than another. No one is greater than another. We all just are. We are all one. We are all learning and becoming more of our true selves the more we grow.

As I prepared to write, my original intent was to create a book explaining how we can make a connection directly with God; how we can hear from God and get messages and how we can use this in our everyday lives to create a better life and world. I had the process mapped out and was working with ideas of how to present it. Plans change.

My family and I had traveled to the family cabin in Northern Canada. We had been there a few days when I felt like I should just start writing. I wanted a title for the book so I could see what direction I was going to go. At that point, it felt like the title was the most important part, as the ideas I was feeling would come together once that was in place.

Our cabin is right on the lake. I walked down the wooden pathway from the deck of the cabin to the dock. My husband was out on the lake with the kids. I sat at the end of our dock, put on some music and breathed in the still fresh air that surrounded me. I began to meditate and connect with God until I heard and saw the words "The Religion of Loving God." It appeared to be written on the front of a leather-bound book that resembled what I think of when I see the Bible.

I asked what this was! "Is this the book I am to write?"

"Yes, and I will be writing this book through you."

"God, you want me to write a book for you??!!!" I asked.

"Yes ... People have many ideas and they share them and they are good, but people do not practice these things until they are written," God replied.

"So, you want me to write for you? How do I do this?"

"Just write what I tell you. You can come to me any time for any length of time, and I will tell you what needs to be written."

"Okay, I will," I responded.

From this point on I meditated and would speak to God but did not start writing until a couple weeks later. My family and I had taken most of our summer that year to go on holidays, so between the business and not having alone time, I didn't get started right away; and honestly, I felt a lot of pressure about writing. After all, it was God telling me to do this!

The day I first took time to sit down and connect with God and write was July 30, 2018. I took it slowly, making sure what I was writing was accurate. I would check multiple times if it was truly God I was speaking to and if the words I had written were correct.

During the writing process, I kept wondering, why me?!! How can this be? I am not a saint. I have lived quite a life with many hard lessons learned. I am not what anyone would consider pure. In fact, if I was to compare myself with other people, I would have been the last person I would have chosen. So why me? I was told it was the reason I came here, to Earth. I did not have to write it, but that had been the plan for me when I came to Earth. I could back out at any time, but this word was needed. If I didn't do it, then someone else could do it. I didn't, however, feel like that was actually ever an option. I knew in my heart it would be me.

I came to realize through this process that we are all equal. We are all deserving of love, no matter how much guilt, shame or feelings of unworthiness we put on ourselves. God does not have any part in any feelings of unworthiness. It is a choice that we make. Unconditional love doesn't hold space for guilt or shame. It only holds space for love.

Prologue

In the beginning was the word and this word was good. The word of truth. This word has been damaged over time. It is originally written that we must desire with our whole hearts the pure love of God. This love is freedom from all the darkness we encounter in a lifetime. This freedom allows us to be in the heart of God. Connecting to this pure love allows us access to the knowledge of all that is. This knowledge benefits us and others and allows our planet to truly heal how it needs to heal.

By the time you read this you will already know this truth deep in your soul, so these words written in this Holy Book will feel familiar to your soul. Peace be with all who read this book. To those who read this book, share that peace with others, as it will bring even more peace.

Turn the page and
open your mind to peace

Chapter 1

Command of Peace

I call upon you now to command the nations to begin practicing peace, or the world will fall upon harder times. This peace is a practice that must be maintained daily forever. This peaceful practice begins every morning and is practiced in the afternoon and finishes every evening. In the past, it was praise that was practiced, but praise (which was intended to bring peace) was not used for peace. So, this new practice of peace is mandatory for the forward progression of the planet's well-being and therefore all its inhabitants. Simply put, practicing peaceful ways daily will change the catastrophic future in which we are currently headed toward, into a loving land of calm and prosperity for all. It is written that man cannot live on bread alone but needs emotional substance as well. These missing emotions of peace, love and well-being have been missing for some time. It is time to change this. It is possible with peace. All things are possible.

This peace I speak of is for everyone. It is not selective. There is no one to be excused from it. This is not a punishment. It is a forward progression for all nations and is necessary for happiness and growth. Detailed in this book is the process used for peace. It is not a ritual but a daily practice to be done three times a day until the focus of the world has shifted from jealousy, hate, ugliness, deceit, crime and injustice, until the world has turned from crying and chaos into peace and love of all. How long this process takes will be dependent upon the nations who choose to be involved.

A command still leaves room for choice. You can choose to follow or choose to continue the current path which has brought so much suffering to my beloved planet and people. Those who love me, follow my command, as they see it is necessary to restore holiness to the Earth.

Just as in the beginning there was a peaceful resonance throughout the Earth, there shall be again in the future.

Let's keep in mind the books previously written for me, the Holy Bible, the Dharma, the Quran and the pyramid inscriptions. All these books at one time were good, but humans practiced praise rather than peace, and messages took on a different meaning than intended. Because of this, this book is to be used only until peace and holiness are restored.* You will know such a time has come when even the fish are happy.

The practice of peace is simple. One must simply focus the heart and mind on loving joy, and peace will naturally follow. It is a simple five-minute practice. Do it until your heartbeat and breathing slow down to a calm, peaceful state. You will always feel better after the practice. If you do not feel better, do it longer. This practice, three times daily, will bring calm, peace, love and joy to you.

This book I give is direct and to the point. The only symbolism [I give] is and should be open to his or her own interpretation, and that can be expressed as his or her own interpretation and not as factual. This is part of the mistakes of the past holy books. There

* (At the time, when holiness is restored, we will be living in peace and therefore not require a book to tell us to do something we already do. The practice of peace will remain. Peace will be a way of life.)

is the truth and then there is the cosmic holy truth, which are similar but almost impossible to understand with the human mind in the way. The truth is only revealed at a soul level, which is what you are being taught to connect to. Once again, this is for your own good. It is not a punishment but an uplifting movement of the spirit. Simply put, to continue on the path of righteousness one must connect with their soul for the answers.

My [God's] heart is full of goodness, as are all human hearts. When you lose the ability to connect with your hearts and therefore your souls, you become weak in spirit. Your desires for worldly needs become stronger than your holiness. This is because of the brain. The brain has set many limits on you here on Earth. The brain wants what it wants right here in this moment, whereas the soul sees what it truly needs.

Your brain is good, but you need a rest from it. This was done through sleep. The energy on Earth has become too strong for some people to sleep. So, the brain needs rest in the day. The practice of peace gives you that rest. Complete the practice of peace three times a day forever. This will rest your brain and bring back the original truth to the planet.

Chapter 2
The Original Truth

You are all becoming light beings, born from the energy of the original light, born to be pure and holy and made of pure love. Time has corrupted your perfection. It is okay to not have perfection. It does, however, hurt. It hurts you and others deeply with wounds your eyes cannot see. It is time to restore your original state of being, and if not to restore, then to remind you of your original past truth. Practice peace in the place of original perfection. This place is beyond your eyes' view but can be imagined and felt with your heart and soul.

Out beyond the stars to the original blackness there was and is a beam of light. It stretches across the universal heavens and has a brilliant warm glow/light.

It contains the original truth. It will fill your soul with light, calm, peace, joy, love and truth. It is here where your soul can be rejuvenated, cleansed and have truth spoken directly into it. Your questions are answered, and your worldly views seem so small. Everything will be okay because this place that resides without you also resides within you, available to you at all times. You are loved. You are loved from the beginning through to the end. You are loved fully without end. No matter what you have done, you cannot determine how much love you receive, as it cannot change. It remains the same as it did at the pure existence of your soul, as it does today. This is the law. It was set forth for you, by you and for your own good. Man cannot live on bread alone. He needs the love of the spirit.

In all storms, you need shelter. My love, the love of the Lord is the shelter. A safe place where you can come to, to know all is okay and wrongs aren't wrongs. They are lessons. Lessons are always good, even if they are hard. You are always loved through your lessons. You never stop learning and this is good, but you need to be loved through learning. That is why this love is accessible for all mankind.

In order to climb to the heights of holiness you must practice peace. [Holiness is freedom from untruths.]

There is no time in space, for all things happen as they will and must happen, when and how they must happen. Therefore, you are not in a rush. The future will unfold itself as it sees best for all mankind.

The world unfolds as a collective. The chaos in the world is collective, so it can be changed. The individual, however, must choose. They must make choices for their future. The world operates on a different vibrational system than an individual. Think of how you feel when you are around someone who feels different than you. They are happy when you are sad or they are sad when you are happy. Think about how that affects you. You have a choice to change how you feel or not. The Earth does not operate this way. By law it changes with the collective. Therefore, the call for the practice of peace is not only important, but vital for world peace. When practiced, the world will follow, as it is the universal law.

These laws are truths of our universal infinity; that cannot be changed. As it has been, so it shall be. Many have seen this power before but not realized where it was coming from. It comes from within the soul to be carried outwards into the expansiveness of the universe. Its works are far reaching, infinite, and doesn't just affect you, it affects you all as a collective.

When people say, you are below the angels, this, in the past, has meant that our abilities to communicate with God were limited. This has changed, and communication can happen on demand now. The channel for this has opened in the last year for all to use. The world collective has been hurting more than it should, and we need this opening to realign within the truth of love and joy.

Chapter 3

The Humans' Will

As young souls, love and joy was at the forefront of your being. Through the years this changed. Worry has carried over from lifetimes through your DNA, so much so that some are born with worry. This can be changed. A planet on edge reacts in ways that harm.

The will of humans is a heavy and powerful burden. The will of humans will prevent your eyes from seeing the truth. It cuts into the soul like a knife leading humans down paths of distrust, untruths, false beliefs and deceptions. A human's will is centered around self, not from within self. Within self, all truths are revealed and appear gloriously before you. It is light and lightweight, and burdens have no part in it.

Apart from the humans' will, you are complete and all knowing. The will of humans began centuries ago. It corrupted your hearts so much so that you have grown to not recognize your own heart's intents and desires. This has caused much pain, and this pain returns over and over, lifetime after lifetime causing despair and weakness in our world.

A time for change is now, to reconnect your hearts and your love for each other. Most of you have never felt this love (this original love) enough to recall it. The time has come to change this. The wounds on this planet are so deep they can only be filled with this love. It is easy and simple but must be done regularly for healing to occur. Think of a needle pricking your finger. It bleeds. It hurts, but it can be stopped. It can't, however, be stopped if you continually keep pricking your finger. Stop the old ways of being and begin anew, in order to heal the wounds of the past. This unfairness we all suffer with has come because of the past ways. The injustice has become a way of life because of humans' will. The system of shame and guilt you have built your lives upon will crumble under the new world laws.

A time for peace is now. In this precise moment, a call for peace is building up in your hearts unlike the world has seen in its history. This will continue to grow daily until it cannot be denied by any nation. Old ways, old orders will become new, and enlightenment will take its place. Calm and peace will be restored, and hopeful hearts will spread their joy far reaching. Kindness and love will replace sorrow and grief, using healing words to comfort those in need and spreading joy contagiously through the lands, until there is peace in the end of the human's war on himself.

Desire for good will far outweigh men's evil desires, and kindness will spread like fire through the lands. Money will not be a source of joy for oneself but a way to help others; and this will be a strong desire rather than a burden or obligation, as it has been thought of in the past. Giving will become a strong desire, until the need for it is no longer useful or needed.

Harmony with all of creation will once again become second nature. Equality of all humans and nations will be shown as powerful, rather than as lacking.

Children will be birthed in love and light and instilled with care and compassion at such a young age that they will never question being selfless. Harmony with all things—plants, animals, other humans, even soils, grains, air and water will become deeply ingrained in us. It will become second nature to care for the well-being of the planet and to show love to the lands and seas and deep waters and skies. The beauty of the planet will always remind you of how Earth has cared for you, and you shall in return care for her/Earth.

Kindness will overcome hardships, as each one belongs to me. The kindness, compassion and caring I show for each spirit and the delicate way I handle each spirit will be repaid. Not toward me directly, but to my own people, which will in return be as though one is showing kindness and caring to me.

I love my children. The young and the old. They are all dear to my heart. When they feel despair, I agonize with their pain. It is those of you who listen to my messages who can reach the hurting hearts and help to make them whole. Not as before when you condemned them and told them they hurt because of their wrong beliefs. We have all felt pain. No one is excused from some pain in a lifetime. Pains are necessary and a means to an end for those who wish to learn and rise up to holiness. Therefore, how much more can those who suffer learn and rise up even higher in their lifetime?

Those who suffer are great in the heart of God. They chose their life to learn for the sake of the planet and those in it. How full is your heart when you can help those in need? Their pain lifts you higher when you are compassionate and they eat the food you helped to provide. Therefore, their suffering in this life is a great sacrifice made for you. How much more compassion do they deserve when their suffering is done for you?

Those who scoff at those in hard times cannot see through the veil in front of them. They believe people suffer because they must want to be in suffering, but that is not true. Their mission, when they were born, was to be a "sufferer." It was a great sacrifice they made and chose to fulfill. They do it for you. That is why you must view every man, woman and child with great esteem and hold them close to your hearts and prayers. Thank them with your heart for their sacrifice done on behalf of you.

When you feel uncomfortable with someone's lifestyle choice, this should gain extra attention and you should turn inward, asking, "How may I help and show compassion?" remembering to thank them for the role they have played in your life. No matter how hard someone has it, you can recall a time when you have played this role for someone else. Be helpful, compassionate and show loving kindness to all.

Call upon the hearts of the loyal servants of God. Bring forth the nations and call into action the peace talks among the leaders of the nations. Practice peace beforehand as a group, united toward betterment of mankind's people. Bring forth the unlimited potential for kindness and compassion, no matter what comes forth from those who refuse to confront the previous evil deeds of mankind. Peace shall promote peace, and only peace shall do it. You cannot promote peace with judgment or prejudice or through retaliation or killing of any kind. Death from the hands of men never promotes peace but only more killing. Be patient, as your views aren't always met with likeness.

Many refuse to see the goodness in mankind. They are blind to goodness because of their own suffering. These are the ones to help by and with your compassion and caring heart, unwavering, no matter the resistance. Continue to care for those who need it most. It matters.

Continually practice peace alone and with those who also practice this peace. Groups of compassionates can accomplish more together than apart. Build a better world, working toward peaceful ways of being together. As a team, create the ideal, judgement-free world we hoped to have. Be patient. Work hard but do not wear yourself thin. To be giving, one must also care for themselves and have time to recharge. This is truly important and promotes peace even further. Your hearts and souls are precious to me, and I love them all equally without change. So be kind and treat yourself with the respect you would expect of God's children.

Chapter 4

I Alone Am God

I alone am God. I alone can bring peace into the hearts of man. I alone am love. This early love is just a taste of the depth of my love for you.* I alone bring this love onto the light of the Earth. I alone have loved you always and without end. I have no judgments to hold against you, which would have kept you from this love. From my view, there is wrong and there is right; but there are also no wrongs and no rights. There just is. And all that is, is good. We see a lion eat an animal and feel compassion for that

* (This early love is God's original pure love. It is perfect, and at one time all humans felt and knew this perfect pure love. This love remains the same, but we as humans tend to forget what this love can do. We, as pure loved souls, could clearly see the purpose of our human existence. Original love has no fears or doubts and holds the knowing that all things are possible.)

animal, but it is not wrong, nor is it right. It just is and is necessary. We hurt a friend and feel hurt and guilt, but we are not wrong, nor are we right. The missing element in any equation that causes pain to us or by us is always love. Therefore, the lack of love is the element we must seek out and watch for. By training your eyes and hearts to spot it, you can fill the need. I alone am God. I alone am love. One in the same. Seek the love of God and you will find it. It will fill you up and make you. The love of God will fill the void in your soul that you long ago forgot you had, only realizing it was missing once it has been filled.

Glorify God by spreading love. Love is all that matters. Learning the giving and receiving of love is the skill to master in this universe. Be kind to yourselves as you master this skill. Be forgiving and loving of yourself and others and be gentle on your soul and others while you learn.

What does this look like?

It looks like too much rain falling on an already soaked field, nearly drowning the crops and causing some rot, but still smiling and being grateful for the rain. It is seeing everything as having the potential for good because of the growth that eventually comes from it.

My dear ones, the riots and wars, the destroyers whom you have followed and been made to follow, this time has passed. For a time, mankind seemed as though his fortune was in power. That power was obtained by greed, killing and the torment of nations, a call to the righteous to heed the ways of those in power who command goodness and fairness. Follow them into peaceful lands. Death brings more death. Destroy a nation and your nation shall also be in ruins. Bring forth peace into the lands and you shall also have peace. Put down the weapons that murder children and the innocent and bring forth forgiveness, love and understanding.

A child left in the cold needs to be cared for, not persecuted when they steal a blanket for warmth, but instead given a blanket, a home and food, care and love. We do not kill this child. We love them. You have killed too many children in my name to which NO deaths have I condoned. I commanded LOVE, not death; my words were twisted to meet the evil demands of humans' hearts. Do not fall victim to your own situations. You have created your situations and are not victim to them. Change. A time for change is now. Create a peaceful future for your children by loving your enemies today. Chaos may fill the lands, but it cannot fill the hearts of those who forgive and love through God's peace.

Begin today with the practice of peace. Begin tomorrow by practicing peace. Begin at the new moon and end at the full moon the practice of peace, a never-ending cycle of continually practicing peace. Do it right now. Do not let a sunrise or sunset pass without having practiced peace. Do not let a new moon rise or a full moon fall without the practice of peace. This is my command for your own good. This is a means to end the suffering and chaos and a move into a phase which the world hasn't seen for thousands of years. Bring forth peace to all the lands and nations, all the tribes and races, all the men, women and children. Bring forth peace. Bring forth the peace that resides in every molecule of the universe. Let its light be shown to the world.

The science of this space is apparent in every molecule. Call upon this space of peace into every living thing that exists in our world. Be kind to all these things. Be kind to all things. Remember you are loved, so loved, but everything is also loved. So, love what I love, which is everything. Open your heart to the beauty of all things and connect to the peace within them.

Chapter 5
The Vision

This is not from God but from the vision giver. I was told the vision giver is a part of God's spirit but not God, the pure source of love. I asked why a vision giver was needed. And God said, "I give messages to different parts of my spirit so that I can remain a source of pure peace and love. I speak to your heart directly and not to your mind or vision center. Therefore, there can be no misinterpretation of my words for the purpose of this holy text." This vision I was told by God to include.

I saw myself covered in a thick blanket of peace, almost like a thick cloud covering. It spread and covered the entire planet. I was told this is the future if we practice what is asked of us. I then saw the cover of peace lift to reveal what was beneath it. I saw joyful people celebrating individually and with others. People brought each other gifts of food and presents as if it was a major celebration. Smiles were on every face and people were jumping for joy, saying, "We did it! We are at peace now!" Cries of joy and shouting filled homes and streets. Then everyone calmed and with smiles on their faces went about their lives with a pep in their step. Jails were empty, now useless. Government buildings were calm, joyful and well intentioned. Corruption ceased to exist. Even the fish in the oceans were happy. There was a deep care for every human, plant and animal. Death still occurred and there was sorrow and grief. The grieving were cared for and groups gathered around to bring them peace. Their hearts were filled with joy toward those who supported them. Peace filled the land with joy in their hearts, and grief passed quickly as the grieving also cared for others. There was community among the grieving.

Peace be with you, my friends, when you uphold the commands given unto you by the Lord of Love.

Chapter 6

I Hear You

I am hearing cries for me. I have spoken to these hearts, but they do not listen. They continue to cry out for me as if they want me to reach down and pull them from this life. I cannot do that. I am sorry. You knew this before you came. Realign yourself with the truth, and life will not be so hard. For those of you who cry out, I hear you. Find me where I reside, in your hearts. Shut your mouths and listen to the truth that is directly spoken to every individual. Learn to have peace in the midst of the chaos. Teach those you know this peace. For those who have peace cannot cause chaos but will be a light to those who have not learned this peace. Pay attention to those who know this peace, for they will lead the way of the future. Your hearts will guide the path to this enlightening. Align your hearts with truth, or you will not have peace. Bring a joyful love into the world with your own heart's alignment of truth. Do not force this onto the hearts of others, but let them desire it to each their own timing.

Call for peace but do not demand it. That is my job. Your job is to love everyone, every heart equally. But do not be forceful, or it will not bring or result in peace. Ask yourself, will my actions or words create more peace? If it will not, seal your lips and hold your hands to your sides as to not create more destruction but to be a beacon of peace. Destruction is not allowed in peace. The old does not need to be broken down in a destructive way, done in the name of peace. NO, do not cause destruction in the name of peace. Peace causes peace and only peace. In peace, there are many elements—caring, kindness, gentleness, love and calm. The opposite of any of these creates chaos. Do not bring any more chaos into this world, but practice peace daily so you may know how to react, respond and help.

Cries for me are heard and responded to. So, practice listening, but this can only be done with peaceful hearts so you can hear my words. Silence the chaos of your minds and hear me in peaceful ways. Be open to many methods of listening to my heart. I love you always and forever. Love me by listening with peaceful hearts.

Create this daily, as the creation of man evolves daily. Therefore, practice many times daily to evolve this peaceful state we all desire. Create this for me so you can all evolve with the need the universe has to evolve. You must be a part of this evolution the universe is yearning for.

Co-existing within the hearts of mankind is the need for love and peaceful behaviors toward others. The heart desires what it wants, but its wants always align with its needs if its focus is on the truth. Create a clean heart of love, joy, strength, courage, bravery, kindness and caring and bring peace into mankind.* You are loved and supported and have the means to do this right now but have forgotten how. Even when outward actions are peaceful, your thoughts can be chaotic, and therefore the results of your actions may not be received as you wish them to be. Remedy this with a peaceful mind and a listening heart, so your

* (God speaks over and over about bringing peace to a deep soul level and not a surface level. When it is said to bring peace into mankind, it is meant to be brought to their soul level.)

intentions can be fully useful to the planet. Call upon me for guidance when needed, and I will hear you and answer always.

The corruption of the planet has been devastating to mankind's heart and soul. The real fear that has been leading you down this road of destruction has caused such great sorrow and grief for my people. The fear has been guiding the wrong path, the path of endless suffering. My beloved children, my beloved children, follow my ways. Follow the path of peace. This means no quarrel is more important than peace. No disagreement takes a higher place than peace. Nothing in the world can be more important to you than peace. Fill your hearts with this peace. It is available to you. Fill your thoughts with loving kindness and you won't be steered wrong. Remember there is no excuse to disobey this command, for it has been set forth by you and for you as well as all mankind. Ignoring this command will bring forth many more devastating effects than previously ever felt.

My commands are done purely and only out of love. You have been blind to the devastation caused in the past. All of this was previously set forth by you but ignored or forgotten, and look at the effects.

Children suffer at the hands of their own unloved parents, and wars so far spread that even the lands suffer. Countries starve their own people for selfish gains. Why have you done this to yourselves? Why choose this? Ask yourself "Are we better off?" Can we move forward without guilt? When will this time end? When will we look back and say, "I can't believe we allowed this to happen!"

My commands in the past were simple but not followed.* More "important" messages were picked out of the religious texts and followed. These were NOT more important. These were lies you made up for your own benefit, to disclude my own people from me. You are all my people, and love is equally distributed to everyone. Therefore, STOP your foolish games and command peace in your churches, your homes and your governments. DO NOT cause wars in the name of peace, for this is also a lie. Peace wins peace, and love wins love. Hate does not win anything. No lessons

---

* (God is referring to those who have taken holy texts and conformed them to fit their desires; leading people astray for their own benefit; creating their own meaning and not the intended meaning; leading people to believe that God is not within each of you. Some of these things were done a very long time ago, but the twisted principals taught are still followed today.)

should be taught by violence, unless you want to raise children who believe violence causes peaceful behaviors. Fear of violence may outwardly cause peace but causes turmoil in the heart, which we want to avoid. Peace, my family. It is simple. Practice peace.

Chapter 7

Darkness Rules Fear

For I will call upon you in the darkness in the hour of the night. I responded to your cries for me, but you ignored my responses. I see your pain, your suffering, your hurt and I am here to help, to assist you. I created the angels. The tribesmen of the past believed in them, and therefore they assisted them. But you have been told to ignore the angels. Some follow them and are helped by them, but you do not. Why have you let fear lead you astray? It is by me that all these things exist. Why should we ignore the angel in the room sent in the light of love? Listen to them, they are here to help. Talk to them in the darkness, when fear is at its peak. Let their messages comfort and care for you. Do not be led astray by those who live in fear. Have you never felt the darkness? It is different than the light.

You can recall a time in your memories when life was good with an even flow. This flow was even and made of light. This is how angels feel, bringing peace, calm and assurance in their messages for you. Darkness does not feel this way. It brings worry, stuckness, fear, grief, hurt and pain. How could you mistake one for the other? Rely on the angels, my love and my light to protect you in the darkness and comfort you in the storms.

Can you not have been with me before and remember my love for you? You forget what love can do for you. You forget there is NO fear in love. The littlest doubt brings forth fear. There are no doubts in my love, it is eternal and everlasting. It cannot change its strength or deviate from the original truth, which is that ALL things were born of this love.

Even the darkness knows the rules of this love. Darkness rules fear. Fear belongs to the darkness. We have been blind for centuries, but this is changing. Do not fear the change, for darkness rules fear. Bring forth excitement at these changing times, for there is much more to celebrate than the changing times but what this means for all of you. Peace and calm previously unknown to man is on its way. Happiness, previously unfelt by mankind, sweetness of life and the deep sweetness of the original truth will be restored to the Earth. Come forth and be a part of this exciting time.

Do not let fear guide you or ignore what I have commanded you to do. First, bring peace back, and excitement is to follow this first change. Bring forth peace and the importance of peace and let love guide the way.

Many of you promised me you would follow my ways until the ends of the Earth. Heed my words now. The second coming is upon us. Bring forth your good deeds now. But do not let fear rule you. Do these things with a kind and willing heart because you have practiced peace and want to. Do not do them out of fear of the repercussions. This is what you have done in the past. It has caused chaos because it was done with an impure heart, done out of self-interests and fear. Erase this fear and fill it with peace. For you are loved, no matter what you choose. For you are loved until the end time, which has no end; and as I said, "My love is eternal and everlasting, even beyond world's end."

Chapter 8

Choose Kindness

Kindness breeds kindness when it is done with a good heart. You may ask "How can this be, that kindness could be done without a pure heart?" It can be done with bad intentions, to manipulate or for selfish reasons. Kindness such as this breeds confusion, dismay and sadness. Woe to you who carry on this way. The second coming will expose your deceit and you will feel much shame and embarrassment, for this is not the way of the Lord. When your heart sees what it has done, it will let go of the old ways and start anew. It will be impossible to turn back to the old deceitful ways. Whatever would cause these deceitful behaviors will be exposed so healing can begin. Do not resist this. Do not hide under a rock afraid to be exposed. Welcome it. For it is the way to the light and true healing for all mankind. Fear belongs to the darkness. Love belongs to everyone, good or bad. Accept this and find peace within it. For you are your neighbors, and your neighbors are you.

Come forth before me and profess your love for me. In doing so you are showing your love for all things, everything made, everything that grows, all things big and small, mountains, seas, grass and air. They have all been made with the element of love. They all respond to loving behaviors. Their core recognizes love and feeds off of it. Be kind to everything that I love. Treat it with respect and a deep gratitude for what role it plays in your life.

Peace is on the edge of every situation and circumstance that has been and ever will be. It has been available, but it hasn't been chosen. It was a decision away, but the choice to avoid peace felt more powerful. Powerful men have avoided peace for eons, choosing corruption, crime, greed, jealousy, revenge and hatred instead of peace. They have their names in the history books as glorious and brave leaders. The time for change is now. No longer will these men have the same appeal as they did throughout history. No longer will we look up to their deeds and glorify their works. We shall feel pity for them instead. Feel pity for their weakness of choices. Peace is always the bravest and strongest act a man can portray. We could all choose anger and revenge. That is the easy road, but to understand and negotiate with fairness and peace takes skill and strength. Therefore, practice this skill and use it, for it provides much strength to all who possess it.

Call unto thy neighbor. Bring forth peaceful unions between you. If your neighbor is difficult to get along with, look at the bigger picture. If we cannot live in harmony with our neighbor, how can we have a united world of peace? Be kind, caring and compassionate. Do not easily frustrate. Practice peace daily so you will want to heal the union between you and your neighbor. If you cannot go into the world spreading peace, then certainly practice it at home and within your communities. Spread acts of kindness throughout your neighborhood with peace in your heart, mind and soul. Doing these acts in love and peace will eliminate your expectations of others doing anything for you in return. Do these things out of love while holding peace in your heart.

Kindness is second nature for those who love God and are not self-serving. Serve God with your heart and bring peace into your wickedness so you can eliminate it from your mind and spirit. Wickedness brings pain into the world. Eliminate it with peace, love and acceptance. Communicate and talk with God in times of trouble. Do this in times of happiness and peace as well. Do this in times of caring and great kindness, as God accepts you, listens and responds, no matter your mood or thoughts. Be aware of avoiding God when you feel ashamed. For this, of all times, is when you can feel God's compassion the most. When you feel undeserving and realize you are still loved is when your soul can truly heal. Do not force these feelings of unworthiness, thinking you will heal more. The damage done is not worth the reward. Delight in happiness, kindness, calm, peace and love.

Chapter 9

Instincts

Trust your instincts. Follow them. This is by design to help you and keep you safe from harm. Do not ignore or shut off these instincts. They come directly from the source of God. Be aware of them and respect them as you would if it was coming directly from my [God's] mouth. Learn to restore this in yourselves. Teach your children the importance of their instincts. Explain it in this way: I [God] have come to you to talk to you in a way that you will understand. I do this through feelings, as to keep you safe from harm. Do not ignore these signs I have given to you, as they are for your own good. Acknowledge them and be grateful for them as to keep them strong and at the forefront of your day. They will not lead you in the wrong direction if you pay attention to them. You can ask "Is this from you, God?" and I will answer you with a peaceful heart so you will know it is I that gives you these insights/feelings. Call upon me and listen for my peaceful response to you.

Chapter 10

Changing Times

Time has always been a vessel for bringing about change. These changes were quite gradual in nature and were correct in doing so. You are never behind. However, change at this time is a must. The direction currently on target is catastrophic. Therefore, a quick change requiring immediate action is needed. This shall bring forth the necessary momentum required to further our existence on Earth with more comfort and ease than noted in the past.

The eras of darkness are coming into the light and shining upon the faces of those who look to seek the truth. What has been hidden shall no longer be hidden. What is right and true and holy shall be brought forward to shine in its ever-glowing light. No longer will you all believe lies or let the powers that be cast their doubt and darkness over you. You shall stand for nothing but the truth and shall delight in it. For you have come to the end of an era of darkness and are stepping forth into an era of truth.

In the past your lives have been drawn to the material existence in which we dwell. Your eyes are now opening to the real world behind the veil of the material. Your eyes are opening to the eternal peace in which you all hold in your future. This process begins today and with you moves forward into the era of truth and lightness. Be kind, oh hearts, to those whose eyes have never seen the light, for their sorrow runs deep. Love them beyond earthly comprehension, for it is those who are lost that need the light the most. Your eyes are the window into the souls of those who are eternally lost. Love them, pray with them in your hearts. Do not condemn them. Do you condemn those who have not learned to walk? Or do you, with patience and love, show them how so they, too, may have the freedom to find their path? Keep strong in your love of the Lord, for it is love that guides the way to enlightenment in the Lord. Be still in the morning and listen to the guidance before you. Hold dear the ones who do not remember love. Shower them in kindness and acceptance.

No change begins in hate. No change begins with judgment of those you love. Rather accept and love and care for those in need. The poor and the rich all have a heart which can decide to love or hate. No one is worse off than another. The age of love, which is upon us, values differently. It cares not for possessions except for possessions of the heart. It treats people with compassion, love and kindness, no matter the weather or the storm. It brings forth open doors to those in need and showers them with compassion and love and care. For those who need, need not ask for help; but those who love the Lord will already be providing for them what is needed. Open your eyes and be aware of those in need. Their eyes reveal the truth. So, compassionate beings needn't even ask, for they shall know the needs of others deep in their being and shall assist in whatever way they can.

Remember, my children, you are loved deeply. So, care for all my children as if they were your own. Blessings shall rain down upon your house for the good you do. I see it all. I see the love you have but are afraid to give. You needn't be afraid any longer, for I will guide your hand to the path of truth and freedom. I will guide you. Follow me to the path of enlightenment in love. Praise the good works of those who do good to spread love with a compassionate heart. Hold them in high esteem so others may be drawn to these works as well.

Bring forth hope to the nations by showing grace to those who are downtrodden. Give to them. Feed them. Care for them. Do not cast blame saying unto them "You caused this and brought this upon yourself." Do not condemn them but show love and mercy, for condemnation comes from a place of hate, not love. Have I not commanded you to love them?

Bring forth armies of warriors that defend my ways of love. There is more strength in love than violence. When did violence ever care for the heart of a man or woman? Violence doesn't care. It condemns. Love those who commit violent acts against you. Correct their ways by way of forgiveness and love. Communicate with their heart, understanding and correcting them by showing their heart an alternative solution to their frustration or hate. Breathe peace into their spirit. For in this way you shall create change and peace without having to speak to them directly, showing them compassion at a meaningful level of their existence rather than at their surface. These are words spoken to the heart, not the ears. Never bring hate nor frustration to a heart. Deal with your frustrations first, then speak lovingly and compassionately into the hearts of those who need it.

Chapter 11

Look with Love

Unveiled, the world's existence appears very different than it does when you look with your eyes. For there is more beauty to behold. There is joy that has been hidden unless you look with your hearts. No matter what your eyes see, your hearts know more than your eyes could ever know. Your heart connects you directly to God, whereas your eyes connect you to what is right in front of you. This is good. You need both your eyes and your heart. Both are equally important, but you have only seen with your eyes and not with your hearts. Unveil the covering on your heart and see clearly my love for you and for all.

Do not be blinded by the shadows, believing there is nothing for you. You shall never see the light hiding in the dark.* Step out, into the light of my love and see for yourself all I have planned for you. See how much delight I have in you, so much goodness I direct to the path of those who love me. Share this goodness with those who need my love. Give to those who need my love. Do not correct them with words from the mouth but with words spoken into their hearts. Meditate on my love and share it freely with all. Be still in your heart and listen, for I will direct your ways. I will lead you toward my love always and forever.

Be kind to those who are little. Be patient. Show them how to love. Teach them the practice of peace, and all things will fall into place for them. Do not do this forcefully but by example of your own practice. Children see and children do. Do not lead them astray to a life of chaos and stress, or guilt shall overwhelm you. Rather, bring your children into peaceful homes and care for them deeply as I care for you. Do not be disheartened and downtrodden, saying, "What if I make a mistake?" There is no peace in that kind of thinking. Practice peace and you needn't worry again.

Love is the answer. It always is the answer. No other answer could ever be as right or complete as

* hiding in fear

the answer of love. Do not dwell on the past, but look forward and answer all questions with love. Try as you might to defeat yourself, it is impossible if you hold love inside you.

Those who are in jail cells see the light of day and feel uplifted. How much more will you be uplifted when you feel the light of love in your heart?

Chapter 12
Harmony

In times past you believed that harmony with all things was not possible. You felt it was a disadvantage to be equals because you believed your greatness comes from being greater than someone or something else. This is, of course, not true, but a difficult concept for you to grasp. You believe that if you are all equal you hold no value or importance. This, of course, is also not true, but a hard concept to understand. Your head says yes, I can see how this would be true, but your mind says, "I need to be better than them or where will my worth come from?" If I am equal with them and I see their faults and they can see my faults, surely my faults aren't as momentous as theirs. Maybe if I have more possessions than them it will make me more important, and I can cover up all my misdeeds. If I am truly equal with the man on the street, then surely I have no value. This is, of course, misguided thinking. For if that man on the street has only love in his heart but no home, does he not have much greatness in him as well? If that man on the street has only sadness and by helping him, YOU could feel valued, does that man not have much greatness in him because of the value he brings to you? If we judge a man by what he has in his possession, then we have missed the point of what is truly valued in a man. What you have forgotten is that love is shared equally. When a child is loved, does it not also mean they are valued? So how could one be more valued than another? It is impossible.

Harmony is not only possible but essential to bring about the change needed. For many, many years the old way was tried and it failed. Have you not learned that selfishness is not done out of love, not even for love of self, but only out of greed and self-importance? Embrace the idea of harmony. See harmony for what it can be and let go of fears about equality making you less important.

When peace fills the lands and harmony fills your hearts, you will begin to experience freedom in the Lord. Your presence becomes a peace to those near to you. Your energy shifts from chaotic to calm and abundant. Your being, being in its natural state, can truly affect the tides in the world with a thought. You can effectively become one collective group of individuals all with the same purpose, to bring more unity, love, peace, calm and joy to your already harmonized world. Bring forth those who wish to follow my ways. Let them gather together to create this change for the good of all mankind.

Fill halls and arenas with good-intentioned people who wish to bring about a peaceful existence in the world. Let their peace fill the cities with a calmness that shall be felt by all. In the midst of war, gather and create peace so mankind will see my ways and be envious of the peace you possess. Then teach them the ways of the Lord of peace and watch as the nations change. Do not be prideful in this gift you possess, for there is no pride in peace. Be careful of those who say they have peace but do not possess its qualities. Do not lead others with a prideful heart, only lead out of a loving heart.

How much more can you accomplish when you feel loved? So, love who you love and love those who need it the most. My love spares no man or woman or child. All are equal, all alike, all beautiful in their own unique way, worthy and deserving of the kind of love that only comes from God.

Chapter 13
I Am Love

To clarify, God is not a man. God is also not a woman, nor a mix of both. I am LOVE, says the Lord. Can not a father, mother and child all love? Of course, they can. This love is neither male nor female, it is just love as am I. In love's sweetness, I accept all. I give all my love in its purest form, which is I. All you need to do is ask and I shall shower my love upon your face, like sunlight on your skin, warm and deep, soft and calm, abundant and without end. Call for me, for I love to be close to you. Feel me in your homes. Take me with you where you dwell. In your body you have made your home. Peace be with you always and forever. My love shall never end.

Cry to me and I shall hear you. Put peace in your heart and feel my presence in your being. For this is what love feels like, pure peace and freedom. It feels like kindness and care, joy, harmony and sweetness, so much sweetness. Come to me and I shall meet you in your hour of need. Come to me and I shall bring you peace. I love you. All you need to do is come to me. I am love, completeness, wholeness, pure and simple holy love.

Gentle rains fall upon your skin, and you are cleansed of impurities. I remind you that all things have a cycle, old and new, being renewed. There is a time for change, a time for cleansing, letting burdens of the past remain in the past, giving time for new experiences to be at the forefront of your lives. Never hold on for too long, or your hands will blister and become painful, unable to keep doing what it is that you ought to be able to do; but let go with a happy heart and embrace the freedom it brings. The time to change is now.

From the depths, I found you. In your despair, I received you. You called to me and I answered you. My love for you runs deep. You tried to abandon me, but my love remains, ready for you when you are ready for me. (The Bible story of the prodigal son comes to mind. It was meant as a story of God's love.) The suffering endured during your abandonment of me was felt in your own heart, and I welcome you back with open arms. My love shall never cease nor grow weak over time, even if you have at one time or another abandoned me. You needn't fear that you may no longer be worthy of my love because of your deeds. For I love you in the depths as much as the heights. Your worthiness remains steadfast and is always upheld. For I loved you before I knew you and always will, forever and always, until the end of time.

You belong to me and I to you. You are my light and I am the sun. You are my peace and I am the calm. Without one, you become incomplete. You are loved beyond understanding forever and again. Love me as I love you, and I will be your light and your peace. Trust in my love for you and believe in my love for you, and I shall shower gifts of light upon your face and soul and uplift your hearts. Trust in my ways, for I will not lead you astray but will instill in you peace and joy to share with all mankind.

Create a peaceful garden in your heart. Daily reflect on my words in meditation, creating peace that will follow along with you wherever you go. Do not resist this peace wanting sympathy for suffering, or your suffering will bring you even greater pain. Choose this peace and follow it, so you can be led down a path of enlightenment. So shall your eyes be opened and the veil be lifted, seeing things as they truly are. For there is great peace in the truth.

Follow my ways and do not lead any astray, for my people need me more than any other substance. Lead them to me with your own peace and show them the meditations of my heart. Bring forth the masses to worship me with their peaceful hearts. The larger the group, the farther the reach of my peace. Calm the mind, body and spirit daily with the meditations of peace. Holiness is in the peace, which is the heart of God. Gentle, like a spring rain, does peace fill the hearts of those I love. Calm and courageous is the peace in my heart. Stand strong and firm in the grace of peace which I have bestowed upon all of you whose hearts seek peace. Love me as I have loved you. Forgive yourself as I have forgiven you. Turn from the wicked ways, as the wickedness brings chaos and destroys your own peace. Turn to the light and follow my ways and fulfillment shall belong to you.

Chapter 14

The Steps Toward Peace

The steps toward peace are simple and shall be followed in this order until further advancements in peace have been established around the world.

Step 1— Start by closing your eyes to limit distractions. Bring calm and peace into your breathing. Do this with the awareness of breath. This shall be done until there is a noticeable relaxation of the breathing and the body. When the noticeable relaxation of breath and body has occurred, then move to step two.

Step 2—Step two can be done in various ways. Whatever image holds peace, security, love, joy and calm for you, use it. Hold this image while you focus on the elements of the image. The feelings of the image, the peace, the security, love, joy and calm of the image. DO NOT get stuck with one image thinking it holds the key to your peace, for many different images can bring peace and calm into you.

While you hold this image count your breaths. Count twenty calm, peaceful, joyful breathes.

During this time, you may have visions or words given to you. Ensure these are full of love, calm and peace. Do not allow any negative thoughts in this positive space, keeping the calm always in mind. When your twenty breaths are complete, hold this peace in you for a while longer. How long you do this doesn't matter.

Step 3—Now spread this peace outward as far reaching as possible. Cover your communities, cities, countries, the globe and beyond. Spread it all the way back to the source of peace, love and all the way to God.

Step 4 (notes in the back of the book)—Connect with God at the place of the light. This is an uplifted place where only light resides and the love of God can be felt directly. Allow this love to be felt, remembered and stored in your heart, mind, soul and body.

Step 5—Give thanks to the creator of this love and light. Then return awareness to the breath and the body. Bring awareness back to the earthly plane.

This shall be done three times daily for your own good.

Chapter 15

Love Each Other

The future of mankind shall be built upon and determined by the ability and willingness to follow what I have commanded you to do. Connecting with me regularly will keep the planet progressing, moving upwards toward me. Failure to listen and to follow what I have commanded for you will be of great consequence for all. During the night, give rest to your bodies which will prepare you for the future you are headed toward. Bring calm and peace into every breath of your day, for everyone has the ability to do so. Eat food provided by the Earth. These foods provided by the Earth are my gift to you and will help everyone restore the balance in their bodies. Treat them with respect and have a gratuitous heart.

Be kind to the Earth and grateful for its resources, and it shall continue to provide what is needed. Do not become greedy and hoard what is provided. Be loving and giving, especially to those in need. Never let another man go hungry while you sit on your pile of food that spoils. Bring peace by giving.

In the end days of this new era, times will become so delightfully peaceful that even the fish and the great whales will be free and peaceful. Their lives will be in graceful perfect harmony with all that surround them. Their waters will be clean and fresh. Their food will be abundant and pure. From the great depths of the sea to the stars in the sky, there shall be a great peace, kindness filling the lands with its vibrant gentleness and peace in the hearts of all who follow me and my ways.

Teach this peace to all, not forcefully but with gentle kindness by being an example of peace to all you meet, to all those you know, to all who inhabit the Earth. Be still in the peace and fully embrace its splendor. Heaven on Earth shall be the feeling among those who love peace. Gather together and celebrate this peaceful harmony you have achieved. Gather together those hearts who seek peace, and as you have been taught, teach those in need. Follow my command of peace and all shall be added to it. Send your love to other nations and assist them in this process, for the whole world needs peace. Love each other.

Chapter 16

*Things to Help with Our Connection to God**

This process may take some time and effort. There are certain things that may block us from the ability to quickly connect to God. These things may be fears, believing we are not capable, that others possess this ability but we do not. There may be blocks that we have put up around us for a variety of reasons, such as doubts or a belief that we are not worthy of this connection; or our own ego or a lack of confidence may stand in the way. To remove the things that may be blocking us from this connection, you must remember these blocks are something you have placed on yourself, not that God has placed on you. So, these are something you can remove. Identify where it is coming from and ask for assistance in removing what is holding you back.

If you believe that you do not have any blocks and the connection for you remains a struggle, then don't worry. You have simply put too much pressure on yourself, and this is what is holding you back. Take a deep breath and let go of the pressure. Think about the pressure draining from your body like water. When the image of water stops flowing (the pressure), try again. Just like when learning to walk, we don't get up the first time, but if we quit trying we will never learn how.

It may be also very beneficial to have someone else lead you through this process: someone who can read to you the steps patiently while you focus on just what is required of you.

Some people may not be able to connect, and that is okay. If you have just practiced the first three steps for one year and had assistance in the process and still cannot connect, that is okay. For those who cannot connect to God after the peace process, this will not inhibit your ability to spread peace throughout the Earth. There is nothing wrong with you. You are loved and you are worthy. Be kind to yourselves.

* (There are to be three more books written at some point in the future. These will be added to this book and assembled as one. When these books come to be has not been determined yet. Questions and answers to this and some other questions are in the back of this book.)

Chapter 17

Extra Guidance

When it is said to connect to God at the place of light, I have seen this place out in the universe. If you imagine the universe and then find a place that is bright and made of only light, just imagine your spirit lifting up to this place. The higher you go toward this place the lighter, more calm and loved you will feel.

When you arrive in this place it may look different to everyone. Don't worry about how it appears to you. When you arrive in this place you don't need to do anything. Just be in that place of peace and love. The more you connect with this place, the easier it will be and the more you will feel comfortable going there.

There is no judgment in this place, only acceptance and love.

In this place you can ask questions and may feel, hear, see or know the answers. Beings may appear, but only to offer guidance or support.

Questions and Answers

Questions based on the future books to be written:

Q: How many more books will be written?

A: Three or four more books, all with different elements in them. The focus of this book is peace. The others to follow will have their own focus.

Q: Who will write these new books?

A: This is not to be known at this time.

Q: Are any written yet?

A: Yes, just this one.

Q: How long until the other books are written?

A: They will be written when and as they are needed.

Q: How will we know they are from you, God?

A: You will just know. You can ask me and I will tell you. Don't have any fear about it.

Q: Will it be me who writes another book?

A: It may be, but it doesn't need to be. There will be many who could write it when the time comes.

Q: What do I do if people don't believe you gave the words to write this book?

A: Just smile and be peaceful. Show them peace and kindness.

Q: How will we know those who still lead your people astray?

A: It is very simple. These people preach on the elements of things in the material world. Their focus is on issues that only matter on the Earth. There are not only no benefits to this way of teaching, but there is harm, as the focus isn't where it needs to be, which is on love.

A: Spiritual practices that are good and true have only spiritual elements as their focus: things such as peace and love, acceptance and kindness. The only benefits of these behaviors are pureness of heart. (This means we do not gain material profits from it.)

Q: What should we do about the misguided teachings still occurring today?

A: Be an example of peace and a beacon of light in the world. Let your face shine with the radiance of holiness. Bring peace and only peace into every conversation you have, whether at soul or surface level.

Q: How quickly can we expect to see a difference in the world?

A: You shall see it within your lifetime if those who choose this peace follow it daily.

Q: What will the first noticeable changes be?

A: We will see peace in the rivers, cleaner waterways. We will notice the new generation that is upon us being very knowledgeable and inspired toward world peace; we will notice their wisdom about this. Natural disasters will still occur in this lifetime, but the way they are responded to will change to a better way. People will begin the steps toward cleaner oceans and air. Wars will significantly decrease. People will still worry, but not those who practice peace; their minds will be calmer and clearer.

46990661R00052

Made in the USA
Lexington, KY
03 August 2019